Men Wan

MW01701051

A Guide to Understanding Your Man

PUBLISHED BY: Dr. Dewayne T. Washington

ISBN: 978-1-964693-08-8

First Edition
Published by
Dr. Dewayne T. Washington
www.dewaynewashington.com

Cover Design: Wanda Daffin
Edited by: Ernestine Rose

Table of Contents

Introduction 5

Why did I Write This Book?..6

The Promise..11

Who is This Book for and Not For? 13

Men are Simple 22

Kid and the King 33

The Three Piece 41

Peace of Mind...42

Be a Geisha 47

Piece of Chicken..52

A Piece of Tail..55

Help! My Man Hates Me! 90

Divorce 98

Cheat sheet on pleasing your man 110

Parting Words 114

Introduction

My official title is Dr. Dewayne T. Washington, senior pastor of the Love Church in Arlington, Texas. But more importantly, I've been loving on the same woman since 1992, so a few decades and four kids later, she still likes me as far as I can tell.

I have been advising and counseling couples for two decades. I've developed a system over the years that has helped married couples stay together longer and have happier, fuller, long-lasting marriages. I've also lived long enough to see what happens when couples totally ignore the training. I've seen what pain and devastation it causes not only in their relationships, but in the relationships of their children and the destruction that is passed down to the next generation.

Why did I Write This Book?

After seeing countless couples and a myriad of different experiences and situations, I have observed two fundamental truths:

1. Almost every marriage goes through the same experiences. The difference is the reaction to it. In every long-lasting marriage there is something that happened in that marriage that also happened in another marriage causing that couple to divorce after two years. There is no "perfect" marriage where everything is rainbows and sunshine every day. If you have a group full of thousands of married couples and you ask those that are happily married to raise their hands, you will see hands go up across the room, front to back and side to side. However, every hand in the building will disappear if you ask those same happy, long-married people how many of them were happy every single day of those twenty or so years. As I stated earlier, my wife still likes me, but over the decades, I'm sure there were sometimes she would have traded me for a ham sandwich.

2. Just about any two people can be married and have a great relationship. This can happen as long as they understand and uphold certain concepts and roles in a marriage, understand the nature of men and women, and CHOOSE to love each other while keeping God first. Just about any two people will be fine.

Over the decades I've noticed patterns in relationships. I'm not saying I can predict with 100% accuracy, but I can say both success and failure leave clues. And over time, we tend to recognize those little clues. I remember a woman being asked when she knew that her marriage was over. She mentioned something very small. She mentioned a particular food she would love to eat, and he would always notice when it was low and picked up more, unprompted. They never talked about it, and she never had to ask. He just did it. But one day, he just stopped. She noticed the first time she ran out. And stayed out. He never did replenish it. He made a decision to stop loving in this way. This was a small clue, but it spoke very loudly, and she was right by the way, at least partly. That wasn't the beginning of the end, that's just when she noticed it. There were years of other clues she ignored. This gesture was closer to the end of the end.

On the other end of the spectrum, a good friend of mine asked his mom when she knew his pop was the one. She told a story of when they were dating. She asked him for some ice cream. He pulled up, she peaked out the window, he never saw her, but he slipped and fell, ice cream spilling everywhere. He calmly got back in the car, drove back to the store, picked up some more and brought it back to her. He never said a word about it. She knew she wanted to marry a man with that type of compassion. Simple, little clues.

Also, once I was in the drive-through of an employee of mine. I pulled around to the window to pay and pick up my food. I was fiddling with something and totally missed that there was a young lady patiently waiting at the window. When I finally did notice her, she was the politest thing ever, and when I realized she had been there the whole time, I was so apologetic, but she was so gracious as to not make me feel bad at all. The exchange left such an impression on me that I turned to my employee and told him, "You may want to get her number." I explained that this is the type of woman you want to marry. She is going to be working the window all day and does it day in and day out. If she can remain this positive and cheerful through the ups and downs (mostly downs) of dealing with drive-through customers, she would make a phenomenal wife, so patient. And that type of patience only comes from the fruit of the spirit. "Go get her number," I told him. He didn't listen. Instead, he found a loud, obnoxious woman who got the police called on him and eventually was the cause of him living in his car. Small things leave big clues, and lead to bigger consequences.

So, what does that have to do with why I wrote this book. More and more I'm noticing that almost nothing in our culture pushes us towards having a good marriage. I've actually seen the opposite. Prior to writing this book, I spent two solid years trying to consume as much info as I could in our current culture on marriage with the express interest in evaluating the quality of advice given both in print and in practice. I had planned on spending five years doing this, but I just couldn't take it any longer. The overwhelming majority of advice in practice and online is not only lacking, but actively pushing people in the wrong direction. I joined countless online marriage groups that were full of people pushing divorce for the smallest of infractions, people just complaining about their spouses, and single people giving bad advice to married people.

The last one surprised me the most. In every married-only group I was in, there was an abundance of single folks giving advice. And it was horrible advice. They almost never would divulge they were single; you would have to go looking or press them for that info. But as a result, real people were taking really bad advice from women with no husbands, and getting rid of their own husband because of it, because he didn't consistently take out the trash, or because they were bored and they "deserved to be happy." They looked at marriage as if the goal is to have a life that is full of excitement every single moment.

I wrote this book specifically to wives and aspiring wives to help them to understand their men, to not over-complicate the relationship and to actually live happily ever after. This book is meant to add my unique two cents to the conversation in hopes that I can help to create healthy marriages and stable families.

The Promise

This book makes a bold promise: by reading it, I promise you will understand your man more fully and have the tools to have a stronger relationship. By applying them it could be revolutionary almost immediately in your marriage. I know this sounds like a bold claim, but it's one I can make with confidence. Over the decades, I have seen these concepts transform marriages in mere hours. I know you are thinking that this is impossible, but remember with God, all things are possible. In marriage, really the only thing that needs to change is a mindset, and that can happen in a moment. The mindset affects everything else, including behavior. The recovering alcoholic who has been sober for twenty years, at some point was sober for twenty seconds, and decided to never have a drink again. If you were sitting in his presence twenty seconds after recovering from being drunk, you may not believe him. But make no mistake about it; it was the mindset for him that changed. It may take years for people to believe him, but that does not change the fact that the mindset changed in an instant. His actions also changed immediately. Once again, the people around him may not have taken him seriously, but that doesn't negate his change. I would ask you to remember that because when a mindset changes, behaviors do as well, but we have a tendency to not believe the behaviors or dismiss them as a fading fad, something that won't last. "Sure, he brought me flowers today, but he will be back to his old self next week." I would encourage you to not destroy your own marriage in the present, with the thought of what may or may not happen in the future.

Who is This Book for and Not For?

If you hate men, this book probably isn't for you. It will be pretty tough, virtually impossible, to attempt to understand that which you hate. One isn't too keen on jumping to love something you despise. It's possible, but not probable.

If you have an extremely physically abusive husband, this book is not for you. While the concepts of this book may help you to understand men better, if you have a man that is beating you every day this isn't going to be helpful in keeping your safe and changing your situation. Keep this one statement in mind. I've never met a man that beat his woman and loved himself. So, if that man doesn't love his own self for whatever reason, he's going to have a tough time loving you, and you will forever be making excuses for him. Dealing with abuse is outside the boundaries of this book. If you fall into this category, we are praying for you, Sis, and please go get some help for this. It doesn't typically get better on its own.

Notice what I didn't say. I didn't say anything about if you have a verbally abusive husband, narcissistic husband, or lying husband. Twenty years ago, I would have included these on the list. But not these days and it's not because they should not be on the list. It's because these terms have been so overused that they don't have the same meaning anymore. I will give you an example. Just this week I talked to a young lady who says she wants a divorce because she refuses to be married to a controlling husband. In recent years, I've learned not to just take this at face value but to dig deeper and ask questions. For example, I would ask for a particular situation that exemplified his controlling behavior. She told me with a straight face that he will not allow her to go out to the clubs drinking without him. She also said that she wanted to take vacations by herself, and he didn't like that. She also mentioned she was tired of having to leave the house at night and explain where she was going. She felt as though this was jealous controlling behavior, she mentioned that she wanted a husband, not another daddy. This is not controlling behavior. As a matter of fact, this is behavior to keep you safe in some of these cases and in other cases, to keep you from doing things you should not be doing and getting into trouble that you should not be getting into. So it is unfair for you to put that all on the man as being controlling instead of you not controlling your own behavior, and in my experience, I have found that in the majority of times when a wife has told me about her husband's controlling behavior, it has been similar to the aforementioned behavior, so I don't include this as a requirement as it has been overused and misunderstood.

Because the word narcissistic has also been used so much, it has also been missed. Many women have used it to mean "I don't like this, I disagree with that thing, I was offended when he said x." The overwhelming majority of the behavior that is explained to me as narcissistic is, in fact, the very opposite of a narcissist. In most cases, a narcissist doesn't really care about you at all or what you do because he is extremely self-absorbed. And on top of that, relatively speaking, there are very few narcissists in the world. However, I have talked to women that will tell me their last five boyfriends were all narcissists, and when I asked them to give me the behavior, it is nowhere near the behavior of a narcissist. We have an excellent example currently in our government. No matter how you personally feel about President Donald Trump, love him or hate him, he is the perfect example of a narcissist. The publication named the Scientific American says he has "extreme narcissism." Let's take a look at the traits necessary for a diagnosis of narcissistic personality disorder.

The first set deals with what they do:

1.) They have an unreasonably high sense of self-important and require a ton of excessive admiration on a consistent basis. How many times have you heard President Trump say, he is the best (insert thing he's talking about) ever, in the world, and everybody knows it. He wants to keep having rallies after being elected president because he loves the adoration.
2.) Feel as thou they as though they need some treatment or deserve special privilege. This man convinced the entire supreme court to give him full immunity, after being convicted of 34 felonies and at the same time convincing the state to just drop the other 50 indictments, just because he's now president.

3.) Make their achievements seem bigger than they really are. You can probably still find clips of President Trump bragging about how well he did on a cognitive test. We get it, you can match shapes and colors, something you only see 3-year-olds bragging about.

I could go on and on with 20 more points, but hopefully you get the picture, you know what you won't hear him do? What John McCain did, praised Obama when a crows try to boo him. What Obama did and called McCain a patriate, when people tried to put him down. He's incapable of praising anyone that is not on his complete and total bandwagon. You also haven't heard him be humble, truly humble, not take credit for something good or take the blame for something horrible. It's always someone else's fault, or if it's good, it's because he's the best president since Lincoln, and perhaps, even better than Lincoln (his words not mine). This isn't a political statement, just stating facts, psychologists around the world use him as a litmus test for narcissistic behavior disorder. So, before you call your man a narcissist, give him the Trump test.

Narcissistic behavior and personality disorders definitely exist, but because other behavior (sometimes regular husband behavior, like saying no it's not a good idea to go on a girl's trip with 5 single women who are single because of their last girl's trip), is mistaken for being narcissistic, I don't include it.

Now let's talk about the last one, lying. While of course I would not have you to use these concepts on a pathological liar, you will have women that accuse their men of being pathological liars when their actions don't come anywhere close to that definition. During the writing of this book, a woman named Nessa Tessa released a fifty-part series explaining what it was like to be married to a pathological liar.

I would encourage you to go watch that on whatever platform you can find it. It's called "Who the F*** did I marry" She does a great job at outlining what being married to a pathological liar looks like. I can tell you this: I've only known a few pathological liars in my life, and they definitely line up to everything she said. One big thing is that EVERY SINGLE PERSON IN THEIR LIFE knows that they are this way. In other words, this man will be lying to every person they have ever met. That includes their mother, father, ex-girlfriends, homeboys, business partners etc. So, if he's only lying to you, not the same sis, even though it may seem like it, but he's not a pathological liar. Has he lied to you? Possibly so, but we will discuss that more in detail later. Why am I even bringing this up? Because it's to say, if your man has lied to you, these concepts will still work. When I talk about who this book is NOT for, I didn't mention those who have a man who has lied to them.

Part of my research included watching different dating shows and there is one particular dating show that I watched extensively. That show was called *Kendra G.* I will talk more on this later, but I do want to mention it here. If you have not seen this internet show, it is quite intriguing and very simple. Kendra will bring on random guests who tell about themselves live while a few thousand people are watching live online. The guests are in their homes or their personal environments and connected with her online. That person will describe his or her life and some things about themselves, and what they are looking for. They also describe what they do not want in a mate. Just about every woman will include no liars on their list. While I fully understand what they meant, I have an interesting fact for you. Ladies, any man that loves you is going to lie to you. I repeat, ANY man that loves you is GOING to lie to you. I know as a woman you may be thinking just the opposite, "if a man loves me, he'll never lie to me." On the contrary, if that man really loves you, I can guarantee he will lie to you. I expound on this thoroughly later, but there is a group of women that I continue to list throughout this book that are a great study for several reasons. They are commonly called sex workers. And I would also include mistresses and side chicks. If you have a conversation with a mistress, side chick, stripper, or prostitute, they will tell you that they commonly get the full truth from a man. The brutal, unadulterated, unfiltered truth. This is because the man really doesn't care about these types of women and has no problem with telling them the full truth. He doesn't care about her feelings or reactions. You often will find a stripper who knows more about the marriage of her regulars than the wife does. This is because the husband has told her the full truth that he has kept from the wife. As with most of the things in this book, I don't ask you to take my word for it. See for yourself. Just find a mistress or sex worker and ask her, or search one out online, they are shockingly forthcoming.

In conclusion, even though I would not advise being with a truly controlling man, a narcissist, or a liar, I do not include these descriptions as the terms have been overly used and misused throughout recent history.

Who is this book for?

This book is for that wife or girlfriend that wants to have a deeper relationship, understand her man better and be able to foster a loving environment. This is for the wife that wants to get into the details of what makes her man tick. The woman with an open mind that truly seeks to satisfy her man. This is for the women who are tired of the dumb advice being pushed by girlfriends, bitter single women and fake gurus. This book is for the women that really want to know what this three-piece is all about.

It's amazing how many books written about how to make men happy are written by women. Although there's nothing wrong with that, after all they are talking to women, I thought it might add to the conversation if you heard it right from the horse's mouth, an actual man.

It should be noted that the contents and concepts of this book have been reviewed by countless men and not one has disagreed, especially with this very first point. Understanding the concepts that are laid out in this book could take you a long way to understanding your man.

Warning: much of the content written to women, written by both men and women, is purposely softened so as to not hurt feelings or avoid approaching touchy subjects. I have opted to not adhere to any of that in this book. Calling you queen every third page isn't going to help your relationship. It might make you feel good in the moment, but you'll still be taking that solo trip to Singapore or eating ice cream for one in that lonely kitchen. So, no more beating around the bush; let's get to it!

Men are Simple

I once sat on a panel of men at a women's conference. The panel included a best-selling author, a professional athlete, an executive director for an international organization, and a couple of CEOs. I looked out on the sea of women and proclaimed three things:

1. You won't be able to walk outside and easily duplicate this group and caliber of men.
2. No man on this stage is about to disagree with my next statement.
3. Men are simple. And that includes ALL MEN.

Immediately, all the men nodded in agreement. These captains of industry and sports gladiators alike were in lockstep with my statement. Want to know who didn't nod and agree immediately? Half the women in the conference. Even though you had every man saying the same thing, many women were reluctant to agree with that statement. There are a few themes that will be repeated throughout this book, so I will mention one here, and it is in the area of communication. I will mention this several times and I want you to think about something. Many women will say the biggest issue with their man is that he doesn't communicate. If you have all of these men on stage, saying the exact same thing, and women still not believing what they say, why would men want to keep communicating? Men are practical creatures and retreat to the area of least issue, so why would they want to keep speaking where they aren't heard? For the women that say, "Well, you don't know my man, he doesn't fit into this category of simple."

Yes, your man fits this category. He's not sone freak of nature that is different from every man on the planet. I don't care about the job position, the title, the education, the experience, or anything else, your man is simple. I have a doctorate, I've been voted man of the year, I was a mayoral candidate for one of the largest cities in America, I started an international youth organization that has spanned 14 countries across the world, I was voted volunteer of the year in Texas prisons, I'm the author of many books, former member of the grammy board, I'm an accomplished musician with several CD projects, I'm owner of a film production company and I too, am simple, very, very simple.

I do realize that after reading this, some women will still say "but you don't know my man." Ma'am, your man is simple, and the quicker you understand this, the easier your life will be. If you still don't believe me, just ask him, go to him and say,

"Hey, Love, I was reading this book about understanding men, and it says the one thing women should understand about men is that men are simple. Is that true?"

WHEN he says yes, believe him. Just this one step of believing him will improve your relationship. We didn't all have a secret meeting to try to trick you. If I'm making this bold statement without meeting your man and he agrees, if you continue to disagree, it's you that needs therapy. Also, if your man agrees without me meeting him, you might want to take for granted that I'm speaking truth and grab hold of the concepts of this book. It might change your life and vastly improve the quality of your relationship.

Some of the concepts in this book are things strippers, call girls, side chicks and mistresses have known for thousands of years, but I'm going to unlock the code for you wonderful wives out there. You may ask, why would I listen to these women? Why would I care what they have to say? These women are experts on men; they have to be. Many of them only have a few seconds to catch the eye and the attention of a man. They have to learn to read men if they want to survive. They have to learn how to listen to men in ways you might find helpful. You may not approve of the profession, but to survive in that profession, they've learned a ton of knowledge that you may find invaluable.

Understanding what they know will answer the question of the wife who, when confronted with her husband's mistress or side chick, complains and says, "I don't know why he would ever choose her. She's not as cute, fine, or intelligent as me." Well, you will get some info in this book on why this is and more importantly how to help prevent it.

Here is a warning as you read this book that you should keep in mind. Everything, every single thing in this book is just like a man, simple. Overly simple, comically simple, but that's dangerous for two reasons.

1. In my experience, most women cannot believe how simple men really are, so they dismiss this advice as not valid. That would be a mistake. No matter if you believe something or not, it doesn't make it less true. If you are hungry and your spouse doesn't believe you, that doesn't somehow cure your hunger problem.

2. Things that are easy to do are also easy not to do. Therefore, it's very easy to ignore the little simple things and discount them as not important.

What they (men) need and don't need...

He Doesn't Need a mom

They have one of those. Whether living or passed on, your man has that area of his life covered. It is the most sacred position and cannot be replaced. Don't attempt to replace it. There are many things that a man would put up with from his mother that he would not tolerate from anyone else. His mother was most likely his first instructor, first teacher, and first corrector. For years she corrected his behavior to turn him into the man you love today. If you say to yourself, well, she didn't do that great of a job, could it be that yours didn't show you how to pick a man properly? Don't try to be his mom! While he respects his mother (and if he doesn't ladies, please run), he doesn't want to sleep with her. And if he does, once again ladies, RUN!

A man needs a mother for their children.

While a man doesn't need another mother, he does in fact need a mother to his children. There is NOTHING that can replace the love and instruction of a mother. A mother's love is the first unconditional love we all experience. It is unexplainable and can only be compared to the agape love God shows towards his children.

They don't need a maid, but they do need a homemaker.
While most men would love to come home to a clean home, it's not the reason they pick wives. Don't get me wrong, being able to keep a clean home is an asset, so don't overlook this, but don't confuse it with a man wanting to marry a woman to dictate the cleanliness of his home.

A man, especially an accomplished man, can hire a maid, as a matter of fact he can hire just about any domestic job, so to think that men want to get married just so they can have a maid is tragically flawed. Men are very capable of hiring help our doing it themselves, and for the things that he doesn't care to do, it is much cheaper and easier to hire someone than to go through the process of marrying someone to do it. And then there are the men who really don't care and are ok to leave in a dirty house with no issue, either way, neither one of those men are marrying a woman for her maid abilities.

They do however need something money can't buy and that is the ability to turn a house into a home, IE a HOME MAKER. Beyond the classical definition of homemaker (one who manages the home) a man is looking for a woman that can turn his house into a home. Put love and understanding and warmth in the house. A man would like a kingdom, but an empty cold castle isn't worth the kingdom. A woman can make a house worth coming home to, but it doesn't happen by accident, it takes work. And if you are saying creating a warm kingdom isn't worth it, well, are you really worthy of being called queen?

They don't need a nag, but they do need encouraging words.

I have some potentially life chaining insight for you here. This may be the first time you have heard this, but do you ever find yourself thinking your teenaged son doesn't hear you, or better still your husband doesn't listen to you at all? Do you feel as though you are talking to yourself sometimes? Have you ever peaked in your son's room and in scolding your son said something to the effect of, ARE YOU LISTENING? DID YOU EVEN HEAR ME? The answer is no, he didn't hear you, he literally did not hear you. Yes, you said it loud, yes you said it in his direction, no he didn't hear you, and you probably taught him to not listen. Allow me to explain using water cups.

Imagine you have an empty cup and a large pitcher of water. When you begin pouring the water from the pitcher into the glass, at some point it will fill up and if you keep pouring the water, the excess will spill out. Imagine it's not water, but words. The average man only has so much capacity to receive words. The large pitcher represents the number of words you have as a woman and the cup represents to the capacity of a man (or a man child) to receive those words. At some point those words are falling on deaf ears, they aren't listening. Men and boys also learn many of these words are empty, so they will move the cup long before it "fills up" and therefore sometimes when you have the tone of fussing, men turn their ears off, and literally don't hear you. So, in a sense you ARE actually talking to yourself when you begin to nag. A trick to this is if you really want them to listen to you, and you aren't nagging, put your hand on them somewhere and then call their name. For example, if you have something of substance to say to your husband, place your hand on his should and say "Greg", you will then have his attention. But whatever you do, don't say, "We need to talk." Just say what you need to say, in a non-nagging way. And if you have questions, ask them in a way that gets you an actual answer. Don't ask him, "What were you thinking when you did this" or "What are you an idiot for doing this" those are good ways to get your husband and child for that matter, to not listen to you, ever.

While they don't need your constant nagging, they will need your praise. Just understand how powerful your voice really is. In a man's life it is quite possibly the most influential voice in his life. The bible even says this of the proverbs 31 woman in Proverbs 31:11 - "The heart of her husband doth safely trust in her, so that he shall have no need of spoil. "A good wife will have the heart of her husband, and once you have someone's heart, you have the rest of them as well. I would submit to you that at times, your voice can be more influential in a man's life than God himself. Hard to believe I realize but think back to Adam and Eve. God told Adam to not eat the fruit of the tree of evil, Eve said here, eat, who did Adam listen to? So, there is no question that a good woman will have influence over her man, the question is what are you going to do with that influence? Are you going to build your man up or are you going to curse humanity, THANKS EVE! But just as your words can be ignored and influence to go against the word of the Lord, they can be also used to build a man up. The voice of a woman is perhaps one of the most persuasive voices in the universe to her man. If you use this properly, you can get whatever you want from your man, and he would be glad to give it. Your words can turn a frown upside down, you can change his mood completely with a smile and a kind word, try it tonight with your man and see what I mean. Increasingly I hear women talk about how tough it is to be a woman, and I don't doubt that for a moment, but have you ever just stopped and really consider what it's like to be a man? A real man? That silently will sacrifice his entire life for his family. That is on the other end of rants and honey do's, expectations and handling other people's pain? Men often have to listen to the woman he would take a bullet for complain that running bath water for him after he just working 2 jobs is just too much, and I wish I was making this up. He has to listen to an entire culture talk about how he is no longer needed (even though all the statistics associated with raising healthy children say the exact opposite). There are no divorce parties for men, only feelings of failure, no consoling. And while women are trying to tell you to express your feelings, you see what happened when Will Smith tried that on the Red Table Talk and ended with memes for days. Consider what it's like to be a man, for real. If this isn't convincing enough, I would invite you to look up Norah Vincent. She ran a personal experiment and decided to live as a man. She received the rudest of awakenings when she actually stepped into that skin. She even attempted to go on dates as a man. She thought as a woman, she would be able to understand and empathize with women much better and wouldn't have any issue in the dating department. She mentions how she was very sadly mistaken, and how tough it really is to be a man, especially with the things men don't even talk about. She lived as a man for 18 months and documented the process. It's an interesting tale. Tragically she ended up taking her own life after this experience, but she did leave behind her findings.

So, ladies, I say all of this just to say, be nice, say uplifting things, say encouraging things. Those words go a long way and help secure that heart I spoke of. A good rule of thumb is saying the things to your man that you wouldn't want another woman whispering in his ear. This way, if that strange woman does try to whisper it in his ear, it won't be the first time he has heard it. Encouraging words from the woman you love is a kind of freshwater spring and breath of fresh air to a man so powerful that I struggle to find the words to explain it.

Kid and the King

Inside every man are two males: a kid and a king. The kid is selfish, petty, mean, immature, vengeful, spiteful and just all-around bad. And then there's the king, a majestic, responsible, thoughtful kingdom-provider. I bet you are wondering who is going to speak to you. It's pretty simple, the one you call out. The one you address will address you.

How many women talk to a man?

I remember once I was running for mayor of Arlington, Texas. As part of the routine, I would go around knocking on doors to talk to citizens. There was one gentleman I spoke with at length. We stood in his yard and had a wonderful conversation, until his girl came home. She hopped out of the car seething. There was no hello or how are you. She just started cussing and being in his face yelling all types of obscenities. Mind you, I'm standing right there. She was attempting to cut his legs off over something extremely minute. She started yelling what to do and not to do in such a way that I was embarrassed for him. She ushered him into the house like an eight-year-old kid who wasn't supposed to have company when his mother was at work, and he has just gotten caught. As I walked away from that house, I couldn't keep from having seen several scenarios. I imagined the story she would tell the world of how horrible he was because he left her for another woman. I envisioned the sympathy she would receive at the hospital and among her peer group when he gets fed up and returns one of the blows, she so liberally dished out to him.

That woman will always get the kid. She will get the childish man that lies and cheats with apparent impunity. That woman will say all men are dogs, all men cheat, and there are no good men. That woman will pull the worst out of any man. That woman is a side chick magnet. The "strange woman" will be able to pick up her scent on her man, she will notice that he lacks attention, proper care. He's dejected, not heard, not respected, and she will make her move. And she will take deadly aim at her man, and the kid will often become a willing victim, all too eager to receive the praise and adoration he has been starving for.

These days, there is no shortage of women who call themselves queens. While it's a great thought and self-esteem is important, it's sobering to remember there is only one thing that makes a queen a queen: and that is her association with a king. In simple terms, every queen is connected to a king in some way. The king could be her husband or possibly her father as with the longest reigning Queen of England. But make no mistake about it, every queen is connected to a king somewhere. Keep this in mind as we move into this next section.

Talking to the King

How to talk to a man

If you consider yourself a queen then you should consider that when you speak to your hubby, you are speaking to a king. While you may be saying to yourself," sure, of course," let the reality of that sink in. Years ago, I took a trip to London. My then fifteen-year-old daughter, my wife and I traveled to the Tower of London and found ourselves standing in an area with some interesting and quite chilling history. On the grounds, we were led about by a beefeater. These gentlemen are special guards on the grounds of the Tower of London and as the beefeater explained, King Henry's wife, Catherine Howard (one of six), was beheaded on the spot where we were standing, in the yard to the right of the tower. Henry the VIII was probably best known for his wives and his quest (and failure) to produce a male heir, mistakenly blaming the women for this misfortune. He was okay with taking their heads off because of it. This was a bit drastic, especially since it was actually his fault, since the male determines the sex.

Why do I bring this up? A man with a bunch of wives and mistresses, some of which he beheaded for various reasons, including giving birth to a girl, would not normally fit into a relationship book, especially one teaching how to better relate to your man. Well, let's take a look at King Henry. I think we can all agree that at best he was uninformed, at worst, an idiotic lunatic. But he was the king, and as such, he garnered a certain amount of respect and obedience. No one stopped him from the beheadings, no one stopped him from the mistresses, from divorcing a wife because she was "uglier than the painting" of her that the king had been sent of her. The reason was simple: he was the king. Period.

We see a small example in the book of Esther where she proclaims she can't just "run up on the king," even though it's her husband. It could mean death. Why is this relevant? How would you speak to someone who had the ability to take your head off your shoulders with one nod and suffer zero repercussions from it? Would you yell in his face while pointing your finger on his forehead? Not if you planned on keeping that finger or that forehead.

I am not advocating that your man takes your head, or that you should be afraid of speaking up. What I am saying is to have a level of reverence when speaking to your man, that is, if you want the king to speak back. But how do you do that?

Ask yourself a series of questions:

1. Would you say this statement to King Henry like that?
2. Could you defend it to God?
3. Would you be ok if he spoke to you like that?
4. Would you want the lunch lady speaking like that to your child?
5. Is there love in it?
6. Is there kindness and tenderness in it?
7. Is there compassion in it?
8. Would you say it like that to your boss?

If the answer is no to any of these questions, then you are acknowledging that your statement is out of line, and therefore you should change it up. It's a shame that many people treat their bosses with more respect and honor than their spouses. Chances are your boss won't take a bullet for you, and if you were to pass, you would be replaced in weeks. Your job description would be online quicker than your family could make arrangements. Don't give your job the best of you and your husband the rest of you.

Learn to be his peace. If that's not in your nature, then find you an aged woman to teach you how. The bible talks of the "aged" woman in Titus 2. This is an older woman whose behavior is coming of holiness and a teacher of "good things." This verse goes on to say that the aged women teach the young women how to lover their husbands. The movie *War Room* has an excellent depiction of this dynamic. There is an older woman in the movie that teaches the younger woman how to deal with her marriage and ultimately how to love her husband. It would behoove you to find a woman like that. She will teach you how to be his peace.

I have had women in my office that say, "I shouldn't have to fake it at home. It's my home so I should be me." First off, if being mean and inconsiderate is being your true self, you need therapy. Secondly, if there's anyone you need to put a face on for, it's your hubby, the one that made a vow to you. You put on a face for everyone outside your home and then when you come home, he catches it? There is an interview with Nikki Giovanni and James Baldwin that exemplifies this perfectly. James says, "If I love you, I can't lie to you ', Nikki says, "OF COURSE you can lie to me! And you will if you love me…. why would you be truthful to me when you lie to everybody else? You lied when you smiled at that (expletive) on the job. Lie to me, smile, treat me the same way you treat him", James replies "I can't treat you the same". To which Nikki interrupts and explains "YOU MUST, YOU MUST, because I've caught the frowns and the anger, he's happy with you, of course he doesn't know you're unhappy, you grin at him all day long. You come home and I catch hell because I love you, I get least of you, I get the very minimum. And I'm saying you know, fake it with me." She then states, "Is that too much of the black woman to ask of the black man?" I'm turning this on its head, is that too much of the husband to ask of the wife?

I'm not saying you necessarily need to lie, but you do need to be considerate and watch how you speak to the one whose hands you have placed your life in, the one who you expect to take a bullet for you.

What happens when you don't?

One of two things will happen if you refuse this advice. A true king will dismiss you for being disrespectful and your home will have one less king in it pretty quickly. The other option is that he will choose to stay and become a court jester while not standing up for anything. That man will probably not catch a bullet for you, that brotha will sidestep and let the perp know where you're hiding! In other words, he'll just stay and become a shell of a man. By the way, this kind of man is subject to becoming fed up at any time. If he is a weak man, he will probably strike you on the way out. Either way, you won't have a king in your home.

Proverbs 14:1
Every wise woman buildeth her house:
but the foolish plucketh it down with her hands.

Don't be a fool. Be a wise woman, use your words to build and encourage a king, not bring out the kid. Remember, as it relates to the king and the kid, you will get which ever one you address. If you come in loud, fussing and cussing, you will most likely get the kid. If you are respectful, and feminine, you will get the king. Trying to be violently conformational with a man can go very wrong, very quickly. There are things men are careful not to say to other men because there is a constant low lever threat of violence. There was a time rapper T.I. was hanging out with his friend Floyd Mayweather, who is a world. Boxing champion. Floyd said something sideways about T.I.'s wife, and the next thing you know, T.I. had punched at boxing legend without of any hesitation, and that's his friend. Things can go left quickly when men are attacked, don't put your man in that situation. Aggression is often met with aggression, but softness will prevail every time, just be soft.

The Three Piece

So, let's get down to the meat and potatoes. This book is called men want a three piece. And also claims that this three piece is the key to understanding your man. What is this three-piece that men want? Well, you asked for it, so here it is. The first "piece" is peace of mind.

Peace of Mind

At the end of the day men will retreat to peace. Peace is defined by stillness and quietness. I don't think anyone would define a rock concert as peaceful for example. When we think peace, we think calmness, stillness. Peaceful waters don't look like roaring rapids. But what does that look like in a relationship.

Many an affair began with a man that was just searching for peace that he couldn't find at home. He wanted the still waters to rest his mind, but he found the battle of the white-water rapids at home. The husband wasn't looking go into the arms of another woman, he was just searching for some peace, a listening ear, a quiet spirit.

It may surprise you that some women of the night report that many times their "purchased partner" for the night doesn't want to have sex; he just wants to spend time. He just wants to talk, and have someone actually listen not judge, not fuss, just listen, just be. In other words, he is paying for peace. You don't believe me? Don't take my word for it. Find a stripper and ask her yourself: Has a man ever taken you in the VIP room to just talk? If you have not talked with these women before, you may assume the answer is no. If you are in this camp, you would be mistaken, it happens more often than you may think. Now I'm definitely not about to suggest that this is the majority of the time, just mentioning that it does happen.

In preparation to write this book, I spent a year diving deep into the popular culture information on relationships, dating and marriage. I soaked up every show, every podcast, every modern book I could find to see what others were saying on the subject and to see if this book is even needed. What I found was a mountain of nonsense and misunderstandings. One show that particularly stood out for me was the *Kendra G Show.* It is comprised of a young lady hosting an online show in which she brings in guests virtually, all at random who have expressed interest. They tell about themselves and what they are looking for. I could write an entire book on this show, every aspect of it was fascinating to me, it is so raw that you see directly into the human condition. It's intimate, these people are in their homes, their environments, and it's pretty interesting. I've also watched the host evolve as well as she listens to the delusions of a woman who has made a lifetime of bad choices, has a string of baby daddies, two diseases named after her and is now wanting a top-notch, perfect man with a 900-credit score who makes two million a day. Kendra went from just letting people say their requirements and moving on, to stopping and questioning women when it seems as though the requirements are unrealistic. Ironically, there was a host named Kevin Samuels that would say the same exact thing, and Kendra was actually a guest on his show years earlier. At that time Kendra disagreed with pretty much everything he said, and now after hearing thousands of women, Kendra sounds like a carbon copy of Kevin, it's quite interesting to watch.

She asks some specific questions, and one of the questions is what are your deal breakers? Almost every single woman will include the fact that they don't want liars. This was interesting to me. Most men didn't mention this on the show as their deal breaker, but almost every woman did. As a woman reading this, you may be thinking the same: of course I don't want a man lying to me. I will tell you this, any man that loves you is going to lie to you, and that's a good thing.

I'll explain. But first, let's digress a little. There is one type of woman that gets told the truth more often than any other. The call girl, The stripper, the sex worker, the mistress, etc. They often get the brunt of the honest truth, the truth about everything. Sometimes they will know more about the marriage than the wife. Because they know about their real feelings in the marriage, how they feel about those kids that aren't his, any weird fetishes, they know it all. These women know stuff your husbands haven't told you, stuff you probably don't want them to tell you. They know the truth, and many times wish they didn't. You don't believe me? Again, find a stripper and ask her. You may think that a stripper would never tell you the truth on this. Again, you would be mistaken, these women live their lives as a pretty open book, literally. But if you don't want to find one in person, just seek one out online. And she doesn't have to be one you contact personally, just take a look at some of the videos of other women talking to them. A good one to search is "What a stripper/prostitute and a Porn Star Can Teach a Wife" which is a YouTube video on the Dr. Gail Crowder channel. And it's just what it sounds like it is. This woman spoke to all three and repots her findings. Or, you always have the option of finding one of them talking on their own channels, once again, they are pretty forth coming. You may not agree with their choices, or their lifestyle, but you should definitely take head on how they grab a man's attention and hold it long enough to get his wallet.

Now, back to the lying thing. Here is an example of how your man will lie to you, every man I know had the same exact thought while watching his baby be born if he was there in the delivery room, but almost none of them voiced that to his wife while she was giving birth, or after And I bet you are dying to know what it is. If your hubby witnessed the birth of your child, then go ask your husband, and if he tells you something sweet, just do this. Give him a huge hug and kiss, put your head on his shoulders and know that he really loves you, because he's lying to you. Strangely enough, the night before editing this book I had a conversation with an old friend of mine and mentioned this, he laughed, and he added, if that man says ANYTHING that makes you smile, he's lying, or at the very least, not telling you the whole truth.

One of the ways you can tell a man is done with you and no longer cares is he will simply stop. Stop what you may ask. He will stop doing something against how he feels. He may even start being brutally honest. I didn't say this is when he is leaving, I said this is when he stops caring. A man can leave you and still care about you, or he could stay and not care at all. Those two things aren't necessarily mutually exclusive.

It may sound strange, why would a man stay in a marriage when he isn't happy, fulfilled, or just doesn't care? Remember, men are more practical than emotional. A man could lose his home, half his cash, access to see his children and still have to pay this woman for the next ten years while some other dude enjoys the home, he put down his life savings to purchase.

That's where the old phrase, "it's cheaper to keep her" came from. I watched a video of a man interviewing a wife. To double down on that, I recently watched an interview where the interviewer asks the woman, "Are you married?" She smiles and says "yes". The interviewer follows up and says, "Is he happy?" She smiles again and says, "That's a weird question, usually people ask if I'm happy." The interviewer responds with "It's a different type of interview…because he's not here, I want to show my care for him as well, is he happy?" To which the woman never answers and almost breaks down in tears. I think we have our answer, either the answer is no, or she didn't care to know, or both. Don' let this be you.

Be a Geisha

Japanese Geisha girls are the ones you will see in painted white faces and colorful dresses at a Japanese establishment. For those that don't know they are actually trained in many arts, some specific to geishas only. They have spent a considerable amount of time being trained to be the perfect companion to a man. They mostly entertain wealthy men, but they aren't just dancers with painted faces, they are trained in the art of conversation. I had the privilege of meeting one and seeing her in action before I knew that's what she was.

I played sax in a traditional Japanese sushi restaurant for about six months, and quickly noticed a particular waitress. She literally floated. She was amazing to watch. It was like watching a female magneto come in and take an order. I studied her for months. I noticed how she treated the customers she would always anticipate a need and fill it before the customer even knew he was going to need it. The drinks were never empty, the table was never dirty. She watched with the eye of an eagle from the corner and floated in like Casper the friendly ghost when the time called for it. Speaking of calling, customers never had to call for her; she was so attentive their needs were always pre-met. After a couple of months of seeing this every night, I expressed my thoughts to the owner. At first, the owner of the restaurant just smiled and uttered two words, "she's trained". It was only after I pressed her for information that I found out what she really meant. This was a true geisha, brought to America, turned waitress, and she was awesome. I remember thinking she will never have a problem getting a man and keeping him happy because her mere presence brought peace. Side note, practicing geishas cannot get married, they marry the art form, not the man.

Learn how to be your man's peace, be the lap he wants to lay in, the partner he can place his trust in, the echo chamber for his dreams, hopes and desires. Be the place he doesn't mind being vulnerable, telling his fears, weaknesses and telling his secrets because he knows he won't hear it again from you or anyone else. Be the place where there is no antagonist, there is no fight... there's just peace. Sometimes it just means being silent. As my wife says, "but we have so much to say." I get it, but sometimes it's about saying nothing

1 Thessalonians 4:11
And that ye study to be quiet, and to do your own business

Simply put, sometimes silence is golden with your man, just be, not say.

You have no idea what the average man goes through and excuses. Chances are he will never tell you. Women often think middle-aged men get together and talk about women and sports and drinking. More often than you think, the conversation will be about life insurance and legacy, knowing they (the man) will probably die first and need to make sure the family is okay. But they probably haven't shared much of that with their wives. About half of what they go through will never be vocalized so just be his peace to let him know that you understand that you will never understand, but you're here for him as a soft place to land.

For those that aspire to be that Proverbs 31 woman, remember
The heart of her husband doth safely trust in her,
so that he shall have no need of spoil.
Proverbs 31:11

What does his heart trust in her? Because she is his peace.

From my experience, there is a good number of women by now that will be saying one of a few things such as "what about me? What about my peace?" Remember this is a book written to women about how women can better understand their men, not the other way around, so putting that in here would not be actionable or helpful, not saying you don't deserve all the same things, that's just a different subject. And there are those who think, that's a lot to do. I'm not doing all that. Actually, it's not a lot with you think about it BUT if you are thinking that's just too much, just know that's fine; there are plenty of women that will handle that job for you gladly. They will take good care of your man. Some require payment, some will do it for free and an ever-increasing number of women don't mind paying for the privilege. In the corporate world, it's called outsourcing. Take your pick. Does this sound harsh? It's because you probably had a man tell you the truth before, so as I warned you in the beginning, I'm going to give it to you straight no chaser, but it's all in love.

If you think that is too much for a wife, it is also probably why a growing number of men are opting out of getting married. Believe it or not, the stakes are much higher for men and the responsibility placed on husbands and fathers is enormous; physically, financially and even biblically. Go take a gander at Ephesians 5:22 to see the expectations and roles of a wife and then read to Ephesians 5:25 to see that of a husband. Then ask yourself, do you really want to wear the pants? Learn how to be his peace.

Here's a hack: next time he's talking to you and pauses, count to thirty before saying something, unless, of course, he has asked you a question. You might find a gem, chances are, after twenty seconds or so, he'll keep going. After he identifies the safe space, you will see communication go to the next level. We tend to think men never communicate, you might find that's not the case, it was you just never gave him the space and respect TO communicate.

Piece of Chicken

Now we come to the second piece. It is said that the way to a man's heart is through his stomach. While many men don't require it these days, there is still something magical about a woman that can cook up a great meal and serve it to you. And I have noticed for the women that can do this, there is a certain amount of pride. Knowing that a man looks forward to an appreciates your cooking is rewarding indeed.

I can't explain this one as well as I would like, but it's the simplicity that brings it all back home. Remember, men are simple. Cooking for them is physically attractive. Serving us the plate is even more attractive. Sometimes serving your man is even simpler. If you think about it, would you be upset if some woman, other than a restaurant waitress, were to bring your man a plate? If so, that is your role. If not, then outsource it, but I will tell you, there is something super sexy about bringing a man a plate. He may never mention it but trust me, he notices.

What should I do?

Does this mean you have to be a former chef? No, find out something he likes, and then learn how to cook it. Men are such creatures of habit, chances are if he likes it at 25, he will still like it at 55. Slowly repeat that process and you will have a happy man.

If you are absolutely against cooking, ask yourself why, because you probably aren't totally against eating! I would ask that you really evaluate it and find out where that's coming from. But if you want to remain with that being, that's fine too. Just make him a plate, even if he cooked the meal. And keep in mind, in general men are extremely easy to please, which means this isn't something you have to do three times a day every day. A little effort goes a long way. This is a little thing, very easy to do, but things that are easy to do, are also very easy not to do. I once had a fellow who I knew would get a divorce after seeing one thing. I never met his wife, and we never talked about his marriage. How, then, can I predict such a thing?

A glass of water.

My wife brought him a glass of water. He was truly amazed, sooo appreciative, too appreciative for this simple act. He was genuinely blown away that a woman would bring him a glass of water. I knew right then; this man is a hungry man! Another woman could get this dude with a glass of water! That's all she would have to do to be special in his life.

I've seen men get divorced and remarried to another woman and be head over heels over this new woman. He'd rave about her, not believing how good life is. In many of these cases it's not that the new woman is some super woman. It's that this man isn't used to somebody doing the basic stuff because the last one was so toxic. He's come to expect a fight around every corner, so when a woman shows an ounce of care or concern, it feels like a breath of fresh air.

When my little brother was in his twenties, he suffered a heart attack. After the doctors went in and put a stint in his heart, he told me how great it felt to breath and that he had not realized how bad it had gotten. That's what it's like for a man as well. Basic things go a long, long way. Keep this one thing in your mind: men are simple.

The last piece is, a piece of… ummm, we will say, tail.

A Piece of Tail

Whenever I am teaching about understanding men in an all-women's seminar, I will ask what is the biggest issue with their men. The answer usually centers around communication, then when I ask them what is your man's greatest need, they all scream out, "Sex!" Well, it seems like men are really good at communicating something, right? Then the question becomes, if you know that, are you taking care of that need properly? There are women that have no issue in this department, kudos to you! For others that think it's not that important or their duty to do so, keep this in mind: sex is really the only action that is sacred to marriage. In some cases, you could say it's one of the only reasons to get married. Everything else can be done as friends or business partners, legally, morally and biblically. Sex is the only differentiator. Of course you don't have to married to have sex, but if you want to do it right and not live in sin, this is the only act that differentiates the marriage relationship.

Sex is a powerful thing that I have never been able to quite fully grasp. It literally opens a portal. For women, it binds you. Think of the first person you had sex with, and then think of how that shaped your attitude and presence towards men. For men, their first sets their preference with women, especially if they remember them fondly. Do you ever wonder why some men are enamored with big women while others detest them? Look at their first experience. That will tell you a lot. And here's a sentence you probably never thought about ladies, a surprising number of men's first sexual encounter was press from the woman to do so. But that's for another book at another time.

Think about sex for a moment, specifically the misuse of it. One bad experience when you are young, such as being forced to have sex against your will, can have negative implications that last a lifetime. Women can have sex with the same man every day for ten years and be bonded and fully in love, while sex with a different man every day for a year will destroy their soul and make them almost incompatible. Why? I can't explain it, but it may be why the Bible has that act between a husband and wife only. I say this to convey the power and sacredness of the act.

These days, sex is taken so lightly, and it's dangerous because the repercussions are more real now than ever before. Spiritual and health concerns aside for a moment, just look at the effect on long term relationships before they even happen. Because of the casualness of sex these days, it is easy to become confused and actually begin to think that sex isn't a man's greatest need. It definitely is. Maslow even put it on the bottom of the hierarchy of needs. This becomes a problem when it is available for free in abundance, then that "need" takes on a different shape. I've talked to countless women that don't understand it's a need. They will bring up the comparison to things such as food, or the fact that men abstain from sex for a period of time. Well, people abstain from food as well, that doesn't make it any less of a need. You would do well just to understand the statement as a statement of fact instead of arguing with a man about his needs, it would be like a man trying to tell you that your cramps aren't all that bad because he sometimes gets leg cramps and he's fine.

As far as needs becoming background because it's in abundance, well, we have a need to breathe, which we don't think about too much until we can't, and then it's the most important thing ever. Sex can be like that for a man. For the first time in my life, I'm starting to see men vocalize that they would want more than just sex. Which makes sense because intimacy is higher on the hierarchy of needs. I even had a young man in counseling say out loud with his own mouth that he wished that his wife would reward him with something other than sex, insinuating that he has had enough of that. My wife still dies laughing all these years later when she recalls my response, which was basically that he needed to hush his mouth. I told him then, he was a newlywed, the sex is going to change, and he is going to regret that statement. He disagreed, and a year later, while complaining about the infrequency of sex with his wife, he swore he never made that statement. He didn't realize how important it was while it was in abundance, but quickly shifted his tune when it became scarce.

Sex is a powerful thing, and the sex drive of a man is sometimes his downfall. Here's a little secret: many men have wished at one time or another that sex wasn't so important, that the below-the-belt brain wasn't so powerful and influential. It can lead you to do some pretty stupid things and is the author of many bad decisions.

Sex has been known to keep you in bad situations a little too long. David had his own soldier killed for it, Samson sacrificed his life for it, and Adam gave up eternity in perfection. The pull and voice of a woman is powerful, mostly because of that sexual energy. Ladies, wars have been fought for over it (see Helen of Troy and the Trojan war). An entire war fought over one woman. Even knew war tactics were created. This war is where we get the concept of the trojan horse from. While you may have occasionally thought of scratching another woman's eyes out over it, you've probably never had the thought of attacking an entire country over it.

Use it, but don't abuse it.

Sex is a weapon. I had an associate once that used to talk about his wife rationing out the goods. We will call it "dinner" for the sake of being PG. You could hear the distain, anger and hurt associated with the statement. And ladies, understand this, if he was willing to vocalize this to some other guys, it's the last resort, and it's gotten bad. Men don't talk like that, we just don't. So, if a man is spilling his heart like this, there's some action that's coming behind it. And he mentioned it not just once, but several times. I knew instinctively what would happen next. At the time, I wasn't a counselor, not a pastor, just a listening ear with enough discernment to know what was getting ready to happen. Fast forward to when I saw him years later, divorced, trying to piece his life back together, he hadn't seen his kids, all because he found "dinner" at the "strange woman's" house.

Simply put, all men want dinner, and are willing to buy the restaurant for it, and most men are even willing to eat at the same restaurant that they own for the rest of their lives. Now really, the men don't want to buy the restaurant. It's expensive, it's risky, you could lose everything. There's no guarantee that the dinner will always be available and as accessible as it seems to be. They just want dinner, but dinner is so good, that they are willing to buy the restaurant, and they will love that restaurant for life. But don't get it twisted. If it didn't have dinner, they probably would have never bought it. Many women may think that men really want to taste a bunch of dinners every week, sampling here and there. Those women really don't understand me, they just believe the stereotypes that others have put out there for men. Most men would prefer dinner in one place, it's when they can't get dinner in that one place that things become an issue.

But what happens when the restaurant stops serving dinner, the one he purchased for dinner? Sure, it has some other features, looks good from the road, nice curb appeal, ample parking, nice lamps and lighting, great ambiance, but there is no dinner. There may be some frustration if dinner is not being served, but let's be reasonable, if the restaurant is undergoing major renovations, getting ready for new customers (having a baby), or is closed due to damage (sick) the reasonable restauranteur understands and doesn't expect dinner. However, when a constant denial of dinner is coming from the restaurant he purchased, and to add to it, there is a new restaurant across the street that has been taunting him to come and take a taste, just a sample, well, it throws a wrench in the system.

See ladies, here's a huge dilemma. When a man hasn't had dinner in a while and he is hungry, it's almost like a bat signal that goes up to women who would love to serve dinner and just don't have anyone to cook for. And these women will undoubtedly approach the man and offer dinner. A good man will want it and turn it down (the first time). I'm going to say that again for the ladies in the back, a GOOD man will still WANT it and turn it down the FIRST time. So let me break this down. I am only going to talk about the proverbial "good man" here, not the player, the abuser, the narcissist, not the compulsive liar, not the perpetual cheater or loser, but instead, the good guy.

The good guy still wants it but will choose otherwise the first time. After the first time, it's all up for grabs. He may hold true, or he might end up having a dinner he never wanted, never wanted to sit down for and he might not even like the food. He just could no longer resist a meal while starving. Many women will say if he loves me, he will never do that. Unfortunately, love has nothing to do with dinner. To quote the great Tina Turner, "What's love got to do with it?" To use real restaurants as an analog, McDonald's doesn't have great food, but it will do in a pinch. Keep that in mind. I've spoken to many women that will get hung up on this and disagree and insist that the two are linked and that love should override. David was a man after God's own heart, he loved God and still slept with Bathsheba, while she was married. Love has nothing to do with it. In the physical, you get hungry enough, you will eat anything, and you don't need to buy the restaurant or be in love with the waiter to grab a quick bite.

I can't tell you the number of wives I've counseled that were upset when their men stepped out on the marriage. But the biggest issue was, "she wasn't as cute or fine as me, or as smart as me." Just as McDonald's isn't gourmet, isn't healthy, isn't that good, what it is, is ready. Just as this other woman may not be as cute, as intelligent, as fine as the wife was, she was willing and ready.

Oh, and please don't let that man have to deal with another man getting the profits from his restaurant that he purchased, while he is simultaneously not getting any dinner out if it. He just might burn the place down. A man that is providing for you, loving you every day and you decide to go and give yourself to another man, that situation is tragic and can be extremely harmful in a mired of ways.

I can hear the comments now. What about him! What about him buying another restaurant? Isn't that a betrayal? Quick answer, of course it is. Now let's think about how difficult it is to own another restaurant vs. you "serving" another hungry customer. Let me take a moment to describe the difference in how both of these are viewed, and why sometimes a man that is able to get with multiple women may be seen as desirable while a woman who has been with many men is viewed as immoral.

Ladies, from the time you were thirteen, men have been knocking down your door trying to get with you. If I were to ask you how many times you have been flirted with in your life, you probably would not be able to give me a number that is remotely close. If you are under thirty, you probably couldn't give me the number of times this week, and this goes for the average woman. You don't have to be a perfect ten supermodel for this kind of treatment. An average overweight woman with a large cup size can post a picture online and get much attention.

Now, compare and contrast. The average man has never been flirted with, except by his wife. I've spoken with fifty-year-old men, average looking, never been flirted with in their lives. Even great looking men, unless they have other attributes such as stage presence, money, fame, etc. chances are the number of times they are flirted with would shock you. Don't believe me? Just ask one. Better yet, ask yourself, when was the last time you flirted with a man? How often do you slide in the DMs unannounced? Chances are, you will notice an attractive man, and your friends will as well, but you won't say a word. If anything, you will wait for him to approach. Just about every woman I have ever spoke to about this has disagreed, including my editor. But when I asked them when was the last time they flirted with a man, I get blank stares, every single time. Well, if you aren't flirting, who do you think is? Have you ever considered what the other side of that is like? Constantly approaching, not knowing what the other side is going to do. Will she accept the advance? Will she decline nicely, or will she attempt to destroy my ego and character? And that's on every single approach! Having to figure out how do I make her laugh in five seconds before she knows my name? How can I gain her trust enough to get the number in under sixty seconds? How can I let her know I'm interested, I'm interesting and I'm not a creep in two sentences. The guys who are the best at this are the ones who do it ALL THE TIME! Think about that for a moment, ladies. If he's smooth, it's because he has plenty of practice and he has figured out what works. In other words, he has skill.

Juxtapose that with a woman. If she has a multiplicity of partners, it doesn't show she has skill, but more like a lack of self-control because all she had to do is say yes with no discretion. Please don't mistake me for saying one is better than the other. I'm merely pointing out why the difference in perception exists. A key that opens multiple doors is called a master key, but a lock that opens to any key is a useless lock.

This is part of why men, in general, view infidelity differently from women. This is why ladies will say it's hard for men to get over a betrayal. What you may not know is that if you check the data, more than twice as many men stay in a marriage after a wife has stepped out than women if a man has been unfaithful. This makes sense since men have a lot more to lose possibly access to the kids, home, credit, and finances. And the thought of another man in the home he used his life savings to purchase can easily create manic behavior. But don't get it twisted; he will NEVER forget it.

The ring in the pocket

Many husbands will privately suffer in silence with the denial of the third piece. Here is another way of looking at it. Imagine a world where rings had the same rules around it as sex does. Now, imagine the most beautiful ring you can think of. And your husband purchased it for you, just for you. You love it, it's perfect! It's lovely, it's your favorite and you know this is just for you. He lets you try it on, and it's fits perfectly. You're excited. Then he says he is going to put it into the box for safe keeping. And he will keep the box on him at all times. But then he stops letting you try it on; he just keeps it in his pocket. You can see the bulge while he's sleeping. I can hear some of you saying, I'd just take the ring while he's asleep. You can't do that. You could go to jail for taking it, and all of society would come down on you for just trying to take the ring without consent.

To add to the mix, every single man on the planet has a ring and many of them are willing to give it to you. You want him to just let you wear it at work, you want to, you like wearing the ring, you would love to wear it, it really doesn't make that much of a difference where it comes from, but you aren't supposed to wear anyone else's ring, just the one at home. But he won't let you wear it. And to make matters worse, your finger is itching. And the only thing that can satisfy the itch is a ring. Truth be told, you are ok with only wearing the ring from your husband for the rest of your life. btw. Now to make a bad situation worse, how would you feel if your husband had the audacity to let another woman wear the ring and not you? You might just smother that brother in his sleep.

Well, ladies, this is similar to how men view sex. The absolute best outcome here is that he doesn't stray; he just resents YOU. Is that the marriage that you want? Your man resenting you? Your man may never articulate it to you this way, but he will to me when he's in my office, or God forbid, to another woman.

And ladies, you don't have to take my word for this. Find a mistress or a stripper and just have an open dialogue about it. They usually aren't shy about divulging this sort of knowledge. They will confirm that these men confide these same things to them. A good stripper believes she could advise the wives of their clients and make herself unneeded, and it's not a question of if she would or not, it's the fact that she could, because she has the info, and the understanding, and the full truth. Think about that. A woman can spend a few moments with him, with a job you wouldn't approve of, and come away with the knowledge to make you a better wife! This is kind of both backwards and amazing at the same time.

Gas station

If you haven't noticed by now, I love analogies and stories because I never know which one is going to stick and which one you're going to relate to. So, I have a lot of them, plus I'm a preacher and that's the way Jesus taught so that's the way we teach as well.

There is a statement that we have all made that is not true. As a matter of fact, we have never thought about it not being true; we all believe it to be true. However, it is not true, and we have all made this mistake. I won't go so far as to call it a lie, but it is definitely not true. Let me explain.

Imagine you are getting ready to go on a long road trip and you hop in the car, and you see the gas hand is dangerously close to E. At that moment, you may say to yourself or even out loud, "I need to get some gas." I am here to tell you that that is not a completely true statement. Not only do we not need gas; we don't even want gas. Allow me to explain. If you were at the gas pump and some gas wasted on your hands, what would you do? Chances are you would rush to the bathroom as quickly as possible to wash the gas off. This means you don't even want the gas touching you. You don't want to smell it, you don't want it on your hands, and you definitely don't want it on your clothes. So, the statement is simple: you don't want gas, nor do you need gas. Gas would kill you. If you ingested it, gas doesn't add to your life. Gas may hurt you by just smelling the fumes, so you really don't want or need gas. But what does need gas is your car. If your car does not have gas, it will not take you where you want to go. So, if you want the car to do what you want it to do, you must first give the car what it needs. You cannot expect your car to go from Texas to Florida and never put gas in the tank. It would be asinine to believe that you could drive across the country without either putting gas in the tank or stopping for some type of charge needed by your vehicle.

Relationships, and I'm specifically talking about "dinner, "are the same way. Many times, we believe our partner does not need or want a certain thing just because we don't want or need a certain thing. And this is far from the truth. This can be extremely detrimental to your relationship.

I have spoken to many wives about their husband's sex drive who say their husbands should not want sex that much. What I hear is my car should not want gas. When you put it in terms of gas in the car, you would never blame your car for wanting gas. You may complain about it being a gas guzzler or brag on it being economical on gas. Either way, you know that at some point on a regular basis, if you plan on driving, you're gonna have to put gas in the car.

I am going to let you in on a little secret. There are plenty of men that wish their sex drive was not that high. I cannot express to you how powerful that drive is. It has the power to override clear thinking, and good decision-making. Good men do not like the power that it wields, and they constantly work to keep it at bay. When you read through the book of Proverbs, you will see there are several themes: there is wisdom, there is knowledge, there is understanding, there are money issues covered and there is the issue that we will call the "strange woman". A good portion of the Book of Proverbs is telling men what woman to pick and more importantly, what woman to stay away from. There is an abundance of writing here and most of it is one-sided to let you understand that there is a huge difference in the way that men and women think and more specifically, the way they each think about and need sex. Even when we look at proverbs 31, it's not written directly to the women, it's words from the King's mom telling him what type of woman to pursue.

Now I am painting with a broad brush. I am not saying that there are no relationships where the sex drive is higher in the woman. I am also not implying that you have this issue in your marriage. There are plenty of marriages that have very healthy sex drives. I'm just mentioning this just in case you are one of many lacking gas for your car.

Now, ask yourself this: if your car needs gas and you pull up to a gas station and the gas station or even just the gas pumps are closed, what would you do? The natural response is that you would drive to a different gas station and unfortunately, that is the path that many men have taken in the past. Whenever their gas station was closed, too many times at home, they simply sought out a different gas station.

I want to make one thing perfectly clear. I am not advocating that men step out on their marriages. We can all agree that infidelity is unethical, wrong, and is against biblical principles. It should not be tolerated or expected in a marriage. It is, in fact, grounds for divorce. However, what I want to bring out here is what sometimes leads to that action. When we see a husband has stepped out on a wife, we immediately begin to blame the husband and say what a horrible person he is and how he should love his wife more. I agree with all those statements. But what I have learned in my decades of counseling couples is that many times, the first injustice was done by the wife. And sometimes, this happens many years before the man responds with something that we all feel should be shunned. But make no mistake. The action is a reaction to the original action of the wife. What I cannot do is guarantee how you have a man never step out on you, but I can tell you how to guarantee that he will. And that is to continue to ignore him and refuse “dinner “on a regular basis. Men will oftentimes tell you when they are “hungry” and if you ignore, or refuse to “feed “this man, that does not make the hunger go away. Not eating doesn’t satisfy an appetite. If anything, it makes you hungrier.

Now this may seem like a lot, and it may seem like I’m dumping on the woman, but keep in mind, I’m only talking to women here. Telling you what your husband should be doing would be pointless and just lead to frustration. You can’t effectively change someone else, but you can change yourself, and many times, that’s enough. Your change can affect the entire environment.

Now, while this may seem like a lot, what am I saying? Three simplified things:

Peace, food and sex. Some would say it this way, Sex, sandwich and silence, and not necessarily in that order. The three-piece. As one comedian put it, "satisfying a man is easy, if he isn't horny, fix him sandwich, he'll be happy for life"

You get your man these three things, and he's probably going to be a happy camper.

And if you are thinking that's a little much, imagine how thick this book would be if I were writing it on how to make any woman happy. And it would be constantly changing, I would have to add addendums daily based on your mood. Men are simple, and consistent. Simply smiling at a man might make his whole week, but you would be surprised to know how relatively few times that happens. What is more common is nonchalant-ness and disrespect. We will talk in detail about this later but keep in mind disrespect will negate everything in this book

But I'm cuter than her

I bring this back up because I've heard it so many times, wives disappointed with the side chicks their men have chosen, as if just being a side chick isn't bad enough. In the decades I've been doing this, I've never heard "Well, yeah, she is a bad one.

I don't blame him for getting with her." Although I suspect some of them thought it, it was never verbalized. What was mostly pointed out are the qualities that could not outshine her own, all but the one that mattered most: the attention of her husband. Again, I reiterate, husbands should not be stepping out, but if this has happened to you, a valid question would be did I leave the door open? Or better yet, am I blaming him for stepping out when I literally pushed him out the door? Now there are men that will eat "dinner" when they aren't even hungry, greedy brothers, but for now, I'm not talking about them; I'm talking about the good husbands.

Proverbs 14:1 says "Every wise woman buildeth her house: but the foolish plucketh it down with
her hands." Don't be the foolish woman, tearing your own house up.

You may say it's too much or you're not in the mood. It's strange how the only thing you are asked to do to be in a married relationship is the one thing you need to be in the mood to do.

Women don't need to be in a mood to do any of these things:

go to work.
change diapers.
wash clothes.
wash dishes.
talk on the phone.
post on social media.

None of these require you to be in the mood and yet you will do them religiously, even though every one of these tasks can be outsourced or eliminated, the one thing you don't want to outsource is the very thing that you are not in the mood to do. Think about that.

There is one thing that has baffled me for all my years and even through my research and interviews, I have yet to ascertain a strong answer in this one area. The most common reason I have personally heard from wives is they are tired, tired when they get home from work. Those that don't work are tired from dealing with the kids. Those without kids or a job will say they're tired from all the housework all day. Those with no kids, no job and a maid will say they are tired from keeping themselves up and preparing plans has them tired. The list will go on and on.

However, a side chick will have three kids, two jobs, must cook every day, clean her house with no maid and somehow still has energy, space and time for whenever your man calls. I have never been able to grasp this. I suspect it has something to do with mind space, but I can't claim to know, feel free to email your thoughts. Info@dewaynewashington.com

I don't want to come off as though I'm attacking wives or assuming you are in this category. There are many wives that do a wonderful job at this and are always trying to get better which may be why you picked up this book. And for those that do, there's someone out there that loves you for it.

You love who you do for, not who does for you

You will hear many say, "We fell out of love." Love is a verb, an action word, a decision if you will. So, no one falls out of love; they decide to stop loving. You may not be totally aware of the decision, but it was a decision non the less. You may also hear people trying to compare love, expecting love to flow both ways evenly, and that's a natural expectation, but allow me to put a caveat on that though with a little more information. We love who we do for, not necessarily who does for us. Women know this inertly, it's why there are men in your friend zone that you would never consider going out with, but you know they will move heaven and earth for you. Chances are you just never thought about it like that.

Think of a newborn baby, who just spent nine months trying to kill you: kicking your ribs, making you sick every day, stretching out your shape, affecting your eating habits and doing a number on your hormones. And yet you are willing to take a bullet for this little joker immediately. Even after he is born, he has no regard for the love you show him: he cries all night, spits up on you, poops on your clothes with no regard at all. He doesn't care that you do for him. You try to negotiate a quiet moment, and he doesn't care. There could be the same response in a teenager, and you can't figure out why he doesn't feel the same way towards you because you do everything for him. Well, that's the answer: you do everything for HIM! We love who we do for, not those who do for us. We typically think the other way around and are confused when it doesn't work out that way. You love that baby in part because of everything you have done for him, not because he does for you.

Want to bring the spark back into your marriage, rekindle the love for your husband, start loving on your husband on purpose? Start making decision to love. The word decision literally means to cut off. Which means cutting off all other options, no excuses, just executing. There are some specific things to do in the back of this book, easy stuff, but very effective. So just remember, men want a three-piece.

Simplicity. “I want what I have always wanted.”
I alluded to this earlier, but men are so simple, even throughout time. Unless sickness kicks in, most wants from your man will stay very consistent even across time. If a man likes a back rub, she’s probably going to like it, at any time, at any interval. Let me give you an example I’ve used in the past to exemplify the difference.

(Ironically my wife just came and rubbed my back :) smile.
Twenty-eight years later, I still dig it. But I digress.

In conferences, I will mention something to this effect. Then I will ask a wife in the crowd, what do you wish your husband would do? These are the most common answers.
Communicate better.
Be more romantic.
Be more concentrate.

I will then turn to her and say, "Hey, man. Ask her what kind of flowers she likes."
She may say white roses, and I will come down and hand him a fifty-dollar bill and say pick her up some roses.

If you think I'm in any way like many of the women at the conference, they aren't impressed. And if he were to buy some flowers, it would mean nothing because I had to tell him. She wants him to come up with that by himself.

Compare and contrast. If I asked the husband the same question and he said a good foot rub, I'd say, "Ok, we have a massage therapist here and I'm about to send your wife in the back to get some lessons. When she comes back in thirty minutes, she is going to give you a foot massage right here on stage." The smile on that dude's face would go ear to ear. You know what he won't say? "Man, I don't want this massage. It's just because you told her to do it." No, that's probably never going to happen.

I've said it once, I'll say it again, men are simple.

Think about the seedy side of life, the concept of a strip club or brothel hasn't changed in centuries. As a matter of fact, the first officially recorded one was 2400 years before the birth of Christ, and I would bet my last dollar the bottom-line mechanics haven't changed much. Simple, throughout time, across generations, across millennia. Even across cities, states and countries.

You can walk into a strip club in Paris, France, Paris, Texas or Paris, Arkansas (and yes, those last two are real places). I'm pretty sure you will witness women taking off their clothing.

Believe what He Says

The simplicity of "man speak" is quite comical. As I mentioned earlier, if I were to ask 1000 women what's the biggest issue in their relationships, the most common answer is communication. If I were to ask those same women what's the number one need of men or specifically their man, they would overwhelmingly say sex. To this I respond, "'Looks like he's pretty good at communicating what he wants at least! LOL!

Imagine you are going on a first date. You two go to a party. After a few moments, you turn to your date and say, "I'm tired and ready to go home."

What does that mean? If you replied, "It means I'm tired. I'm ready to go home," then you are consistent with the overwhelming majority of women to which I have posed this question.

I would like to pose some alternatives. Could it possibly mean something else?

1. You aren't having a good time.
2. You don't like the vibe.
3. You don't quite feel safe.
4. You see someone you don't care for.
5. You don't like this date.
6. You like this date a lot and want to get out of here and spend some one-on-one time.

See how this can be confusing for a man, especially those last two, being completely opposed to each other? This is why the man is completely thrown off when you mention half-way home that you'd like to stop and see a movie. Men (especially that new husband you may have), will believe you and take you at your word, poor guy. Seasoned men have learned the hard way: you might not mean exactly what you say.

You can probably see where some disconnect could exist, but with that being said, it's not the thing that causes most of the issues.

Take the same scenario and the man says, “I’m tired and ready to go home.” Chances are, he’s tired and ready to go, that’s it. The problem comes when his date doesn’t hear that. What she hears is he is not having a good time, or she thinks does not like her. She may wonder it’s something she said when there’s nothing to it.

There are times when a wife has called to set up couples’ counseling and given a doomsday scenario, he hates her and is leaving tomorrow. The man comes in and has no idea what she’s talking about. He just said he would be late from work because of a project, but she wants to know if she can come sit with him while he finishes. Nothing remotely close.

You will find that if you simply take a man at his word, you’ll do well. If he says he doesn’t want to go grocery shopping, it doesn’t mean he hates you and wants a divorce. It means he doesn’t want to go to the grocery store.

Y’all give us much more credit than we deserve. Most of the time, we simply aren’t that deep. Again, men are simple, including your man. He’s simple, too. You don’t believe me? Go ask him.

The Ten-Year Argument

One thing that used to scare me was the fifteen and twenty-year-old marriages that were headed to divorce court. Then I realized one thing: relatively few things happen twenty years into a marriage that cause it to crumble. They crumble because of something that happened in year three that somebody never got over. They might have just been waiting for the kids to grow up. Who knows? But chances are, the issue isn't new.

Now, let's look at how to deal with a man who is unhappy, and it's been a while. He may have even threatened to leave. I will ask, what's the ten-year argument? What is the one thing he has complained about for ten years? And if you are not careful, he will stop complaining. This is dangerous and it's the beginning of the end. This is where he has stopped trying. He has thrown in the towel and no longer has faith that things will get better. He has resigned. You may not notice it, because quite honestly, it might seem peaceful, but there's always calm before the storm. Men will continue to provide every day during this period, but don't get it twisted, they have already left in their heads. If you find yourself in this situation, you may want to home in on what he is saying and respond. It's usually something simple.

It's said that men don't communicate, but just as the greatest need example, it's apparent that not only can men communicate, but they can do it very well. Why don't men communicate more? Because men have gotten a lack of response, been ignored or even mocked in some cases. They've learned to stay quiet and not to put their feelings out there. Men retreat to peace. Next time you are wondering why your man doesn't just open up, Google the Will Smith crying meme on the "*Red Table Talk" show*. There you have your answer.

Just look at how much hate Kevin Samuels got for basically saying this is what men want. The average man doesn't want to take that much heat and drama, so he says nothing. What you may not realize is most men think congruently to most of Kevin's thoughts. If that triggers you, then that is the reason men don't communicate. What's the benefit? It's easier to lie to you and avoid the drama, or better still, keep it to himself.

When he stops complaining

As I mentioned earlier, this may seem like bliss when a man finally shuts up about something he has been complaining about for years, but it's the canary in the coal mine. It's a signal that something has died in the relationship and there may be other things to follow.

Years ago, I was listening to a talk radio program, and they were discussing, well, "dinner" and serving "dinner" at home in a marriage. A woman called in and said how she had been married over ten years and her husband would often mention he would really like more "dinner". It was a constant point of contention, and she mentioned about six months ago he stopped complaining. The hosts went silent; every man listening knew what that meant. When the host finally put a statement together, one of them just followed up with a question: "So, why do you think that is?" Her response "I think he's just finally more in touch with my needs." It's like I could hear the collective thoughts of men listening across the nation, "Poor woman. She hasn't the slightest idea!"

It's a misnomer that men don't communicate. They will just stop communicating when they deem it's not necessary. They stop communicating either because of lack of trust, lost hope that the situation will get better, or just not being sure the information won't be used against me later. If a man doesn't trust you, he will not communicate his whole heart, he will be reserved. Likewise, if he doesn't have confidence that you will start listening to what he has been saying, he will lose the will to continue to say it.

Respect over love
Ephesians 5:22

If we read Ephesians 5:25 written as instruction to a husband and compare it to Ephesians 5:22, there is an important word missing. The Bible calls for husbands to love their wives, but you don't see the commandment for wives to love their husbands in the previous verses. Don't take this to mean that love isn't important. Titus 2 instructs the older women to teach the young women how to love their husbands, but it also implies how important it is for you to reveal and respect your husband. On the scale of importance, most men would place respect higher than love. In a Boolean scale, where you only have two options like on or off, most men would choose a woman that respects him but didn't love him over a woman that loves him but is disrespected to him every day, especially in public.

If you can't figure out what respect is, imagine disrespect and do the opposite.

Cussing him out in public--- disrespectful. What's the opposite? Talking sweetly to him in public.

Telling his mama she raised a fool--- disrespectful. What's the opposite? Thanking his mother for raising her husband.

Now, you might be saying, "But my husband is a fool! You could be right, but in the statement, I didn't say if he was or wasn't a fool, or if he was raised well or not, just thank his mother for raising him. And you want to be careful about calling him a fool because he managed to get you, and I'm assuming you believe you are a catch, whereas all you could get is a fool. Tread lightly. I bring this out because again, in the last couple of years I've seen countless sessions bashing men, and it seems like there are two things these ladies are failing to grasp.

1. There are other men watching this. You are turning off all the good men and attracting the same types back to you.
2. Men will look at this and say, "Why were you with a fool so long? Seven years? Three kids?" Women will retort, "He fooled me." Men know that very few men

> are capable of that level of trickery for that long, so they just see you as the stupid one if you can be tricked by an idiot.

It's like I told a kid once who complained that his teachers were imbeciles. I told him that may very well be the case, but they hold the key to his future, and if you can't figure out how to get your key from an imbecile, then who's the real imbecile? The first imbecile's already gotten their degree.

It may be a tough pill to swallow, but I gave you the warning at the beginning of this book. I'm giving it to you now, straight now chaser.

NEVER HIT A MAN WHERE HE IS WEAK

In my course on marriage training, there is a module on fighting fair. That module discusses the different types of fighting styles couples often use. The most lethal of all is the one-shot, one-kill, or the sniper approach. In simple terms, this is when you hurl a carefully crafted insult at your partner in the area that you know he is weak, where it will have the deepest impact and do the most damage. Their Achilles' heel, so to speak. This insult is so specifically aimed and placed that it is sure to shut down conversation, induce pain and there's no coming back from it. In other words, hitting them where they are weak. I advise you NEVER to do this, especially to your man.

In a relationship, as people open up to each other, they are basically handing their partners weapons to destroy them. This could be telling each other about childhood wounds and past hurts or grievances they have and fears they've picked up along the way. With this you are handing your partner an arsenal of weapons that could be used against you. True lovers never pick up those weapons. If you choose to hit a man where he is weak, he will never forget it. And I mean NEVER forget it. He may never mention it, but don't be fooled into thinking he forgot it, or he has gotten over it. I've seen many men leave a twenty-year relationship after his kids got grown and the wife seemingly has no clue what happened. But when that man is questioned, it sometimes comes down to that injury that was suffered years ago. It never healed, and he just bided his time until his children grew up.

One thing to remember is to never hit a man where he is weak, no matter how upset you get. No matter how disappointed you become, he may never fully recover from it. Take it from the long list of wives and ex-wives that have tried it before you.

So, what if you already went there? You need to have an apology session immediately, and be specific on the apology, not just “Hey, I’m sorry.” No, you should be very specific. I am sorry I said THIS. I was wrong about that. I never should have said this or done that You may be thinking, but I don’t want to bring this up. You would be surprised at how much he thinks about that; he just hadn’t mentioned it to you. You may say, “I don’t want to open old wounds,” but chances are that wound is much more open than you realize.

Help! My Man Hates Me!

If you are reading this and you're thinking, "This is all well and good, but I believe my man hates me," then you are facing a more serious problem. Here are a couple of scenarios that are at play.

1. You have over-exaggerated this in your mind and have literally made this up. In other words, no one hates you, it's all in your mind. No one really thinks this is the case, but I can assure you, sometimes it is.

3. Your man is upset with you. He doesn't hate you, but he is displeased with you. You may have done something or said something he doesn't appreciate, and he's probably communicated that to you already.

4. He hates himself.

5. He does hate you. This is the worst scenario. Chances are if he hates you, you know for sure. He will treat you with distain and wishes you weren't there. Sometimes only staying in the house some financial reasons, or possibly the kids.

If you want to figure out which situation you are in, it's simple. Ask him. Tell him you feel like he hates you. Most likely he will say something to the effect of, "I don't hate you I just hate what you have done." At that time, don't make excuses, just apologize and talk through it. There could also be a situation where he is feeling unfulfilled within himself. This is tricky because while you can support this man, you can't force him into loving himself. Usually, his affirmation with other men needs to do this. If unfortunately, he says I hate you, you have a serious problem. It's worse you say you don't know why.

The one you want and why he won't commit to you

To my single sisters out there, have you ever thought to yourself, why is it that the ones I want don't seem to want me and the ones that want me are not the ones that I want? To you have an abundance of guys in your friend zone that you couldn't imagine being with, but at the same time can't seem to get that certain someone to look your way, or even know that you have a pulse. Have you ever looked at the men who are interested in you and thought, they just aren't my type? Has it ever occurred that maybe we shouldn't even have types? Think about it for a moment, in general, a type is what you have been used to a technically what you are ‘attracted to” but for the most part we are attracted to what’s familiar. If you grew up in south Dallas you may not be “naturally attracted” to someone from south India, or the Philippines. It probably has less to do with attraction and more to do with proximity and familiarity. But take that further, if you are single, chances are your “type” isn’t working out to well for you. Could it be that you have been conditioned to be attracted to that which is bad for you because of familiarity? Could it be that we shouldn’t have “types” to begin with. It means that you have had multiple relationships with the same “type” that didn’t work out. Maybe it’s time to do a little soul searching, a little internal work. Perhaps it’s time so some introspection to find out why you are led towards the flame like a moth.

How to know he’s still interested…

You may want to know how to tell if this man is still interested in you or not. Sometimes you may think that the man you are with or the one that you’re married to is no longer interested in you. One good way to find out is to simply ask, “Are you interested in me?” You’ll find that surprisingly that is oftentimes the most effective way. Many times, women are scared to ask the question, because they don’t want to know the answer. I say all the time, if you don't talk it out, you'll act it out, so you may as well have the conversation. Do men lose interest over time? Sometimes, but usually not just because of time. It's a result of the woman that he loves, ignoring his needs, wants and feelings and unlike women, they will stop mentioning it, and simply slip away.

There was a woman whose video I watched, she told of how great of a man she had. He was attentive, thoughtful, intelligent, emotionally available, understood and spoke her love language. She said it was a dream come true, the perfect man. Then she mentioned after about 2 years, things begin to change. He didn't talk to her as much, he wasn't as tentative to her and eventually he left. Many women will look at this and say, that was his representation showing up for two years. I'm here to tell you, it is very unlikely that he faked it for two years, men have a hard time keeping up a facade for two months, much less two years. Upon deeper investigation it's what I suspected, while he was doing all these things for the relationship, she was not returning any of these things, he got fed up with the one-way relationship and decided to move on. Moral of the story, just ask him.

But also keep in mind that I said at the very beginning of this book that a lot of times a man that truly loves you may lie to you. And if he loves you but doesn't like you, there is a chance he may try to spare your feelings, and not tell you that. So, what do you do? First off, watch his actions. Men may not always be big on words, but most times they are big on action. Does he do special things for you? Does he treat you with respect? Does he care for the things that you care about? So, watch his actions toward you and see if they have changed. If his actions toward you have changed, in other words, they used to show compassion and now they don't, then you may want to have the hard conversation of what is happening. Don't readily assume that he is doing something behind your back. Be generally inquisitive of anything that could've changed in your relationship, including what you may have said or done. This is not to say that nothing is going on, or you should tolerate bad behavior towards you. I am nearly saying seek first to understand, and then seek second to be understood. You may have done or said something inadvertently to change how he feels toward you and the quicker you can address that, the better your relationship will be. You may say that you don't want to do all of that, to which I would reply, "Why would you be in a relationship that is not worth saving?"

Men are like water: water flows to the lowest point, men retreat to the lowest level of conflict. In other words, men retreat to peace. Many a man have been destroyed because of just trying to retreat to peace. Sometimes men retreat to work or throw themselves into a hobby, other times the retreat isn't so innocent.

Men will retreat to all types of peace:

1. The side piece
2. The liquor at the bar
3. The strip club
4. Drugs
5. Violence (This doesn't sound peaceful but that's at his core… think about deer hunting, quail hunting, fishing, etc. Success equals death for something, or destruction.)

I've seen men get 30 years in prison that started with them just trying to find peace. I've seen men get hit with assault charges that were originally looking for peace. Addictions of all types, drugs, alcohol, sex, and pornography to name a few. Remember you hold the keys the door of peace for your man, it's up to you if you choose to open the door or leave it locked.

Now when men need peace the most, many are being raised without other men and fathers in their lives and in general are being raised in an environment that is much more hostile to men in general, is when they are getting the least. There is a movement in the west for women to say out loud how men aren't even needed while simultaneously wondering why they can't find a date. Increasingly I have been asked by women why they can't find anyone because they have all the success attributes. They have the job, the money, the cars and the houses. The thing is, while these are great accomplishments, it's not something men really value in women. This are things WOMEN value in MEN, but not the other way around. For example, imaging if a man has 300 pairs of shoes and purses that match every outfit. Would that be impressive and attractive to you? Keep that in mind, things that you find attractive aren't necessarily the same thing people may find attractive in you.

Common myths and misconceptions about what men value in women:

1. Men care about your job status.
2. Men care about your education.
3. Men hold out for beauty queens (the baddest girl will be home on prom night).

4. Men are intimidated by women who earn six-figures.
5. Men grade women by the same type of criteria as women grade men.

By now, you've probably heard this before, but let's look at why. Many women would love to have a man who is taller, stronger, makes more money etc. And if possible, would like to have the choice of whether to work or not. Which means, no matter how much you have, most of it is off limits to the man. In other words, in most cases, your money and status won't help him much, and if you have "status" you will pick a man with much more "status" and would change your situation anyway. I have a friend who married a very accomplished woman. She had recently purchased a new car, when he proposed the very first thing, he did was replace her car, stating that everyone with his last name drives this kind of car. So even though she is accomplished, he still used his resources to replace the vehicle.

Common myths and misconceptions about what women value in men:

1. Looks don't matter (a 350-pound woman is not the same as 150 pounds.).
2. High value men represent all men.

3. Thugs equal protection.
4. Wealth equals love.
5. Bad boys are good for you.
6. There is an unlimited supply of men.
7. Daddies don't matter.
8. Marriage equals happiness and fulfillment.

Divorce

Men and women need each other. When there are problems, divorce should be the last option. Prior to getting married there are two things I knew for sure:

1. I had no idea how to be a husband.
2. But I knew I didn't want to get a divorce.

Up to that point, I had never seen a good marriage. I was pretty sure what a bad one looked like, and very aware that divorce is a viable option for a lot of people. It was almost a staple in my family. So how was I to be something I never saw? How was I to make something work without a manual? How could I build a great life without blueprints? Simple, I needed to go get the blueprints. Even though I had not seen a good marriage, it didn't mean that it didn't exist. Because of this revelation, I went on a three-year fact-finding mission. I must have talked to a thousand people who were or had been married. Everywhere I went, I would ask "Hey, how long have you been married?" or "I'm getting married. Any advice?" There are several things I learned from this exercise. First off, I learned A LOT of people had gotten a divorce, like, a lot. Even the people I met that had been married thirty years, some of them joked that they got it right the third time around. At first glance, you would assume that it's all about marrying the right person, which can make you very gun shy. How do you know you have the right person? I was eighteen; what did I know? How would I know how to pick someone to spend the rest of my life with when I can't even legally pick out a drink in a bar? While there is some truth about picking the "right" person, it isn't as daunting as it may seem. First off, the "right person" isn't the "only" person, or your "soul mate". While this sometimes happens, it isn't necessarily the best option, or even a necessary option. After being married now several decades and training other married couples for over twenty years, I now believe almost any two people can be married successfully, granted they follow a few rules and understanding some basic ideas about marriage.

So, what did I learn? First, let me give you the ranges that I spoke to in order to lay a foundation. They primarily fell into seven groups:

Married 20+ years

Married 10-20 years

Married 5-10 years

Married under 5 years

Married and divorced within 1 year

Divorced in 7 years or less

Divorced after 10 years +

There was something unique about each group. However, the last group, the folks that have been married 15, 20 even 25 years and then get a divorce, this was terrifying to me. It thought after a while you would be on easy street! And there was also something very interesting in those that I queried, and it was a sizable sample. When the marriage was an older marriage, then divorce was often filed by the man, which was totally different from all the other categories that were dominated by women.

And the reason was consistent in that there was usually a ten-year-old argument. This argument is over something this man has been unhappy about and has expressed this same thing to his wife for ten plus years, and then suddenly, he stopped complaining. This is about the time his youngest child hits his or her teens. The wife doesn't notice. She may even welcome the peace, but this is the calm before the storm. At this point, he has decided. He understands that his wife isn't interested in the solution, for whatever reason. She doesn't care or just isn't interested, but it's definitely not because she doesn't know. It is at this point that he has decided to leave, but his youngest child isn't old enough yet. In my findings they will wait until that child is between sixteen and eighteen before they leave.

There are several reasons for this. At sixteen, that's old enough for them to be raised, the man feels they will be okay, and it's close enough to eighteen. In general, he wants to wait until they are eighteen, but sometimes he cannot wait a moment longer and he decides to bounce. That man is the HARDEST man to get back into the house because by the time he physically leaves you, he has mentally left you years ago. He has already grieved the relationship and moved on in his heart and mind. He believed nothing would ever get better no matter what he said, so he stopped saying anything. There are some warning signs, though. A huge one is moving out of the room. If a man has left the room, he has left you, and he probably left you two years ago, but if he is still in the house, it is salvageable. Be forewarned if a man says these terms:

"I've told you this a thousand times."

"Why can't you just listen when…"

"How many times do I have to say…"

"I'm getting tired of saying the same thing…"

"What I'm asking is simple, just…."

I would also ask you to resist the urge to say, "But what about him? What about when I want him to XYZ?" That won't help you here. This book is written to you as an instructional guide of what YOU can do. Plus, you would be surprised at how much the atmosphere changes when a man feels heard. If you are five years into that ten-year-old argument, in other words your man has been complaining about the exact same thing same thing for 5 years. Or he has been asking something of you for five years. Don't let it make it to ten, instead nip it in the bud or you may find yourself by yourself in those golden years. Also, things are changing, men are talking, and when that young man hear the old man talk about it didn't change after 10 years, they are less likely to make it the whole 10 these days.

Every long-term marriage has been through something similar to what another couple has divorced over. This is an important thing to remember. We will often try to compare our marriages. Maybe it's to the happy couple on Instagram that seems to always get along (#RelationshipGoals). Or possibly, it's the couple next door that always seems to be traveling together. "Oh, if we could just be like them!" you may say. There is a reason the bible says that we should not covet our neighbor's' spouse, partly because you really don't know your neighbor's situation. And every marriage goes through something that another marriage got a divorce over.

How romantic to see the 85-year-old couple holding hands in the park, that have been together for 65 years! However, upon deeper inspection, there are probably about ten years of that marriage where the wife would have traded that guy for a nickel and given back change. The thing to remember is that you will go through something, every marriage goes through something, and for the most part, they all go through very similar experiences. The difference is the response to conflict. Don't immediately think because this one thing went wrong, you need to run down to the courthouse and file for divorce.

I made it clear at the beginning of this book that this book is not for you if your spouse is beating you and you don't feel safe in your own home, by all means, take care of yourself, I am speaking to the other issues. I've heard all types of reasons these days, financial (as if you will suddenly be rich once this other person leaves), not romantic enough, no communication and my personal favorite lately, I'm just bored. No love, you are stable, and you have become accustomed to chaos, so stability feels slow and unfamiliar. I will issue a warning to you if you are in this category. A stable woman who feels bored is probably the in the top category to have an affair. On the surface, this may not make sense, why would a woman in a stable loving relationship consider risking it all for an affair?

But when we look a little deeper if makes all the sense in the world. We all know the female mind works different than the male mind. Most times, much more active. A woman who is in a relationship with a toxic partner, who is always lying, manipulating, gaslighting, and belittling her is also literally filling her mind. She won't have the mind space to cheat. You can think back in your own history or the history of your friends, have you ladies ever cheated on a good man and stayed faithful to a jerk? Well, this is part of the reason why. This isn't an absolute and definitely not the only reason to cheat, but it is definitely a major contributing factor.

If you find yourself bored in what is a stable relationship, it's probably a good sign that you need therapy. There is some trauma in your past that you have not only normalized but come to expect. It would behoove you to explore and correct that. The trauma may not be your fault, but if you choose to hold on to it and wreck your relationship, that is definitely your fault.

Foolproof Way to Stay Married

Once I was in a restaurant waiting to be seated. I ran into an older couple that had been married longer than I had been alive. I asked, as I always do, what is the secret to being married that long. The older gentleman said he had a foolproof way of staying married as long as he had been married. He asked if I would like to know. I said of course. He told me to come close so he could tell me the secret key, so I obliged. As I got closed, he said, the key to staying married this long is to not get a divorce. We both laughed but over the years I had though more and more about that statement. That statement is truer than it appears to be at the outset. It may seem obvious, and you can easily dismiss it, but let's dive deeper. There is not a marriage that had lasted 25 years that hasn't experienced something that the couple that split up after 2 years has experienced. They have all had something happen in those 20 years that another got a divorce over, whether it was as simple as misunderstandings all the way to infidelity. The big difference isn't what happened, I've seen the 20-year marriages that went through much worse than couples who got annulments. The difference is the reaction to whatever has happened. The ability to forgive and reconcile. Verses just calling it quits. That's something to think about in your relationship.

Why Side Chicks Be Winning

Years ago, there was a stigma attached to being the other woman, the side chick if you will. That stigma has disappeared. There are plenty of women who not only will sign up for the position but will brag on it with no intention of becoming the "main chick." They are perfectly content with just borrowing yours. We've even heard hit songs such as "The Weekend" in which singer Sza proclaims "Your man is my man too…. You take Monday - Friday, I just keep him satisfied through the weekend" …" You like 9-5, I'm the weekend" …" Make him lose his mind every weekend." Ladies, I can't stress what a dangerous time this is. There is no more scarlet letter, these women are making hit songs about the position of side chick. Don't make it easy for them. In my life I've known some very interesting and talented young ladies. Some of them I was truly glad I was their friend and not their victim. I personally watched how they targeted men who were taken by girlfriends and fiancés. They caught those significant others slipping every time. These women had the exact same tactics, and to sum it up, the M.O. was just to cater to the man. If you want to know what that means, go pull up the lyrics to "Cater to You" by Beyonce. The definition is clearly laid out in this song, and these women would basically just do that. The sad part is that it worked every single time. But they also explained to me the REASON it worked. It was because it's not difficult to have a hungry man accept your food. They say you can lead a horse to water, but you can't make him drink. Well, if that horse has been deprived of water for 8 days and you've been feeding him crackers all day, you don't have to force him to do too much.

So, specially, what are these women doing that the wife isn't?

They focus on one thing, being his peace. Whatever that means

They are available

They build up his ego

They act like they believe in him

They make him feel important

They don't belittle him

They cater to him

They let him know they want him (when was the last time your man heard that from you?)

Women mistakenly think that the men that fall for this are just weak, or don't want to be kept or don't love you. That's about the equivalent of a man saying if she loved me, she wouldn't nag and fuss. Many women will also say, well if it's that crucial why doesn't he just leave? The answer could be a complex one: Maybe for the kids, possibly he doesn't want to lose half his stuff, and more often than not, he loves his wife and has no intention of leaving, she just doesn't lift a finger to satisfy his sexual needs. So just as a woman may think a wife not sleeping with her husband doesn't give him grounds to seek it elsewhere, understand him stepping out also doesn't mean he automatically wants to leave his wife, any more than the wife wants to leave the husband just because she isn't having sex with him.

Expectations

When it comes to disappointments, they are rooted and grounded in one thing: expectations. You can probably trace every disappointment to an expectation not met. Whether it was a reasonable expectation or not, makes no difference. For example, if we were to meet and I hand you an envelope unexpectedly with 10k in cash you might be excited. You were not expecting that, so by default it exceeded your expectations. However, if prior to that meeting I promised you I would have a briefcase with 1 million in cash for you, the 10k is a letdown, because the expectation was not met.

In your relationship, at some point you will be disappointed in your spouse. You may say, pastor, you should be more positive, well, I am positive, at some point you WILL be disappointed by your partner. It's not a question of if, but when. The bigger question is what you are going to do about it. The natural thing is to get upset and blame him. And for right now, I'm not taking the severity of the disappoint into consideration, because I've seen divorces over the silliest of reasons. But human nature will have you to feel that hurt and want to project that back on the person. We say things like

"How could you"

"Don't you know how that made me feel"

"You're so inconsiderate"

"You make me sick"

"Why can't you just listen for once"

"You should've known better"

And the dreaded

"You always…." or

"You never…" fill in the blank.

There are times you may want to (correction) will want to choke this man, and not understand why he can't see things your way. In those times consider he may feel the exact same way, and the way you would want him to respond, try that approach on yourself.

Cheat sheet on pleasing your man

Here is a quick list on pleasing your man, don't think about this stuff, don't try to refute it or try to over rationalize or dismiss it. Just do it and see what happens.

1.) Listen his dreams, and encourage him

2.) Look in his eyes for a good 20 seconds, and wink

3.) Learn to give a good massage

4.) Text flirty text

5.) Text sexy texts

6.) Serve him dinner and an apron, only

7.) Call and talk dirty in the middle of the day

8.) Show up to his job with lunch

9.) Lay in his lap and say nothing

10.) Rub the back of his head while he's driving

11.) Learn the art of fellatio

12.) Learn to cook his favorite meal

13.) Give him a foot massage, wearing a lingerie

14.) Actively work on not nagging

15.) Read the book, the proper care and feeding of husbands

Say these things, again, don't try to over analyze them.

1.) I love you

2.) I'm proud of you

3.) You make me want to do better

4.) You make me want to be a better wife

5.) I'm proud to call you my husband

6.) I missed you today

7.) You make me feel safe

8.) I love the way you take care of me

9.) You are the best

10.) You're the best lover

11.) I can't wait to make you a father

12.) I care about you

13.) You're so handsome

14.) (wake him up to this text) good morning handsome

15.) I feel safe when you're around

16.) I appreciate you

17.) Come here

18.) Hurry home, I have something for you

19.) You're smart

20.) You matter to me

21.) You mean something to me

22.) I believe in you

23.) You are so amazing

24.) I want you

25.) I need you

50/50

Frequently in dating circumstances you hear the 50/50 question. It's usually talking about finances, are you willing to go half with a man, or should the man pay for everything. This is such a bad and backwards way to go about a relationship. I've lived lo ng enough to see plenty of end-of-life situations. I watched my mom take care of my stepfather till the day he died. She did such a wonderful job; hospice was not needed in the home. He was there on his back, unable to do for himself. I watched my grandfather take care of my grandmother till her last breath. In relationships there are ebbs and flows. Marriage is never 50/50, in anything. It's not even an intelligent conversation. Marriage is far beyond finances, but even in finances, there may be times when one spouse is sick, or going to school and the other is holding it down. There may be a situation where one is starting a business while the other holds down a corporate job to make sure there is a steady paycheck and benefits.

Marriages aren't 50/50 in anything. I can promise you that there will be times it is 60/40, 70/30, 100/0 and 110/-10 (somebody isn't even trying to do right). There is the concept of what do you bring to the table, why don't you pick someone you can build a home with, along with the kitchen and the table.

Marriage isn't transactional, it isn't a business, it's not a contract, trust me, I've got many businesses, many partners, but only one wife, and there is a difference. Instead of looking at how tall a person is, or what is current job status is, look at someone who will be holding your hand when you close your eyes for the last time.

Parting Words

Throughout this book, resist the urge to want to point the finger at your man. There's the whole, "but what about him." It's a natural thought, it's one I've heard many times, but again, I urge you to resist it. You may be tempted to say but what if he's abusive etc. strangely enough the abused woman doesn't need to read this book, she's probably already submissive, she has a different issue, so chances are if you picked up this book, you aren't getting your head smashed in every Thursday, and if you are, out this book down, get out and call the authorities, you need some safety and healing, not the words of this book.

Resist the "but he" temptation. Men are simple creatures who don't require much. Understand and do the things outlined in this book and watch how he changes. But don't do these things with expectations, less you will quit after a week.

I wrote this book for one reason, to help marriages. To help them to exist more often first of all and to exist in a more harmonious way. This book is written specifically to women because many times women are so influential that just you changing will change everything. As the old saying goes, if mamma ain't happy, ain't nobody happy. And believe or not, if you picked well, your man really just wants to please you.

When you start doing the things in this book, you might just find your relationship go to new levels and it might just feel like you have a new man. Good luck.

Made in the USA
Columbia, SC
20 April 2025

56867543R10065